21ST
CENTURY
DEBATES

KT-572-703

FOOD SUPPLY

OUR IMPACT ON THE PLANET

ROB BOWDEN

an imprint of Hodder Children's Books

21st Century Debates Series

Air Pollution • Endangered Species • Energy • Climate Change • Food Supply • Genetics • Internet • Media • An Overcrowded World? • Rainforests • Surveillance • Waste, Recycling and Reuse • Artificial Intelligence • Water Supply • World Health • Global Debt • Terrorism • The Drugs Trade • Racism • Violence in Society • Transport and the Environment • Tourism • New Religious Movements • Globalisation

Produced for Hodder Wayland by White-Thomson Publishing Ltd,
2/3 St Andrew's Place, Lewes, East Sussex BN7 1UP

© 2002 White-Thomson Publishing Ltd

Published in Great Britain in 2002 by Hodder Wayland, an imprint of Hodder Children's Books
This paperback edition published in 2003

Produced in association with WWF-UK.
WWF-UK registered charity number 1081247. A company limited by guarantee number 4016725.
Panda device © 1986 WWF ® WWF registered trademark owner.

Project editor: Kelly Davis
Commissioning editor: Steve White-Thomson
Proofreader: David C. Sills, Proof Positive Reading Service
Series and book design: Chris Halls, Mind's Eye Design
Picture research: Shelley Noronha, Glass Onion Pictures

British Cataloguing in Publication Data
Bowden, Rob
    Food supply. - (21st century debates)
    1. Food supply - juvenile literature
    I. Title
    363.8

ISBN 0 7502 4454 2

Printed and bound in Italy by G. Canale & C.S.p.A., Turin

Hodder Children's Books, a division of Hodder Headline Limited, 338 Euston Road, London NW1 3BH

Picture acknowledgements: Ecoscene 38 (Alan Towse), 41 (Christine Osborne), 57 and 58 (Wayne Lawler), 59 (Ray Roberts); HWPL 28; Impact Photos 13 and cover background (Chris Moyse), 5 (Francesca Yorke), 12 (Erol Houssein); Panos Pictures 4 (J.C. Tordai), 6 (J.C. Callow), 10 (Heldur Netocny), 18 (Zed Nelson), 20 and 33 (Betty Press), 22 (Dominic Sansoni), 29 (Nancy Durrell McKenna), 45 and 52 (Fred Hoogervorst), 56 (R. Jones); Popperfoto 35 and cover foreground; Still Pictures 7, 8, 31, 32, 42, 46 and 54 (Mark Edwards), 9 (John Isaac), 15 (Jim Wark), 17 and 27 (Hartmut Schwarzbach), 19 and 21 (Ron Giling), 23 and 44 (Joerg Boethling), 24 (Nigel Dickinson), 26 (Thomas Raupach), 36 (Peter Frischmuth), 37 (Robert Holmgren), 49 (Gil Moti), 51 (John Paul Kay), 55 (Nicholas Granier); WTPix 43 (Chris Fairclough).

Cover: foreground picture shows a young malnourished boy gathering his share of grain left by a World Food Programme air drop in the village of Akon in Southern Sudan; background picture shows supermarket shelves in the UK.

CONTENTS

A HUNGRY WORLD

'Even one hungry person is one too many'
Jacques Diouf, Food and Agricultural Organization, Italy

Hunger in a world of plenty

Some of the world's 850 million hungry people being fed at a Red Cross feeding station in Baidoa, Somalia.

At the beginning of the twenty-first century around one in seven of the world's population suffers from undernourishment – better known as hunger. Not the type of hunger you might feel as you pass a pleasant-smelling restaurant, but real hunger. Hunger that makes you so weak you barely have the energy to move; hunger that makes you vulnerable to disease and threatens your health; hunger that prevents you studying or working. So why then, in the last century, did humankind fail to end such hunger when it succeeded in beating several killer diseases, raising the standard of living for millions and even sending people to the moon?

The truth is that we have not completely failed. We actually began the new millennium with more food than ever. Between 1960 and 2000 world population doubled to 6 billion people, but world food supplies increased even faster. In fact, the amount of food available per person increased by almost 20 per cent. How then can we have a hungry world when we know there is plenty of food to go around?

An unequal world

The problem, most experts agree, is not a shortage of food, but who gets what. This can be measured by looking at the number of calories a person receives per day. Calories tell us how much energy food gives us and we each need about 2,500 calories per day. In poorer developing countries the average food availability is often less than 2,100 calories per day and as low as 1,585 in Eritrea, North-East Africa. In wealthier developed countries, by contrast, people consume an average of over 3,200 calories per day. Denmark has one of the highest calorie diets at 3,808 per person, almost two and half times more than an average Eritrean. This shows that, although world food supplies have increased, they are not shared equally. In reality the situation is even more unequal, as these figures are just averages. This means that some people receive a lot less, while others have a lot more.

*People in wealthier countries are becoming overweight,
such as these tourists in Trafalgar Square, London.*

FACT

Globally, the average number of calories received per person per day rose from 2,336 in 1970, to 2,751 by 1996 (an increase of almost 18 per cent).

FACT

Obesity is responsible for at least 250,000 deaths in the USA each year and is the second biggest killer after tobacco.

Local markets are a vital source of food in many developing countries. Here, Nigerian women sell surplus vegetables near the northern city of Kano.

Feast or famine

Global inequalities in food supply mean that some people feast on luxury foods every day, while others face the constant threat of famine and starvation. Famines occur when food shortages last for a long time. They are often linked to droughts – low or failed rains that cause crop failures and livestock deaths. However, a country or region can experience drought without famine. In Uganda in 1999, for example, a drought in the north and east of the country was managed by moving food from the south and west where supplies were more plentiful. Countries may also use stores of food, but sometimes they have to appeal to the international community for help. Some of the worst famines in recent years (in Ethiopia, Sudan and Somalia) have been due to wars and conflicts. These disrupt food supplies by damaging infrastructure (roads, railways, food stores, etc.) and forcing farmers to abandon their land.

Whatever the cause, millions of people die every year due to food shortages. However, millions more suffer and die because they have too much food! In the USA, Germany and the UK, for example, over half the population is overweight. Weight problems cause ill-health and early death for millions every year. So if there is enough food for some to feast, surely we can avoid people starving to death? Unfortunately it's not so simple.

A difficult future?

If there are problems with feeding everyone now, what will it be like in fifty years' time when there are nearly 3 billion more mouths to feed? Scientists tell us that new technologies such as genetic engineering and improved farming methods will enable food supplies to keep up with population, but at what cost? Some environmentalists argue that genetic engineering may be dangerous and could cause unforeseen problems, while others point to the large areas of cropland that are already overused and suffering from soil erosion and declining fertility. Whatever happens, food supply will become an increasingly difficult issue in the future. This book explores some of the questions that will have to be answered.

Modern farming methods, such as the use of combine harvesters shown here near Perth in Australia, have increased food supplies but at a cost to the environment. In Australia it is estimated that 7 kg of topsoil are lost for each kilo of bread produced.

VIEWPOINTS

'Even developed countries are confronted with the challenge of overcoming food insecurity.'
Jacques Diouf, Food and Agricultural Organization, Italy

'Hunger in wealthy nations is neither as severe nor as widespread as in developing countries.'
Marc Cohen and Don Reeves, Bread for the World Institute, USA

FACT

The diet industry in the USA was worth around US$50 billion a year in 2001.

DEBATE

Try eating less than you normally do for lunch and see how long it is before you feel hungry. How does it feel and how does it change what you do? Now think about what it must be like to be really hungry. *Warning!* Do not starve yourself and tell an adult what you are doing and why.

TOO MANY MOUTHS TO FEED?

The population explosion

Three hundred years ago the world had fewer than 1 billion people, most of them farming the land for their own survival. At about this time improvements in farming techniques enabled humankind to produce more food than was needed (a surplus) for the first time in history. This surplus was one of the factors behind the start of the Industrial Revolution in Europe. It released people from depending on the land, instead allowing them to work in industries and buy food with wages or in exchange for manufactured products. Scientific and medical discoveries during the nineteenth century enabled humans to thrive and by 1900 world population had increased to 1.65 billion. But it was in the twentieth century that human population really began to increase. In fact it was increasing so rapidly in the last half of the century that many referred to it as a 'population explosion'.

These Yanomani Amerindians living in Venezuela find food in their natural environment and cause minimal damage. As world population has increased, such systems have broken down.

Too many people

By the mid-twentieth century the world's population was about 2.5 billion and it reached 3 billion just ten years later, in 1960. Scientists began to warn that there were too many people and that the planet could not support such large numbers. If nothing was done, they said, millions of people would starve because of food shortages. They were not the first to make such predictions however. In 1798 Thomas Malthus wrote a famous book in which he suggested that population increased geometrically (1, 2, 4, 8, 16...etc) while food supplies could only increase arithmetically (1, 2, 3, 4, 5...etc). He predicted that this would inevitably lead to food shortages and famine or even war as people fought to have enough to eat.

Terrible famines in India, Ethiopia and elsewhere during the 1960s, 1970s and 1980s, in which millions of people died, seemed to confirm that his beliefs were correct. And population continued to grow faster than ever, reaching 4 billion in 1974, 5 billion in 1987 and passing 6 billion in October 1999. However if Malthus' theory was true, why weren't millions of people dying of famine in 1999, when the population was double that of 1960?

The 1984 famine in Ethiopia was so severe that only healthy children with a chance of survival were given food. They were marked with a cross on their foreheads.

FACT

With the right amount of water, sunlight and chemical inputs, HYV crops can be planted and harvested three times in a single year.

Scientists in the Philippines infect a new variety of rice with the disease Sheath Blight to test its resistance. Such testing has helped increase food supplies significantly since the 1960s.

Feeding more with less

In reality global food production has kept pace with population and the number of major famines has decreased over the last thirty years. Much of this progress has been achieved by growing more food on the land available, a process called 'intensification'. World grain production, for example, increased by 124 per cent between 1960 and 1999, while the land area used for growing grain increased by just 7 per cent. In other words, production (or yield) per unit of land more than doubled over the same time that population doubled, thus avoiding the mass starvations that had been predicted.

Intensification was made possible by new crop species known as High Yield Varieties (HYVs). These are improved grains (cereals) such as wheat and rice that are specially bred in laboratories to produce higher yields than traditional species. Their impact on world food supply has been dramatic – in fact so dramatic that their introduction during the 1970s became known as 'the Green Revolution'. Pakistan and India were threatened by famine in 1965 when HYVs of wheat, and later rice, were introduced; within ten years they became self-sufficient in grain supplies. But HYV crops are not without problems. They demand large quantities of chemical fertilizers and pesticides to grow successfully, and they require expensive irrigation in areas of low rainfall. These 'inputs' cost a great deal and poorer farmers often can't afford them. Some have been forced to sell or give up their land to wealthier farmers and work for them instead. However, work can be scarce, as machinery and chemicals have also replaced many human jobs such as planting and weeding. And the increased use of irrigation and chemicals can damage the environment.

Regional variations

Despite the increase in global food supplies, the pattern has not been even between regions. The chart below shows how the calories people received each day in different regions changed during the period 1965-1995.

VIEWPOINTS

'The green revolution may have increased yield in its narrowest sense, but its main effect was to widen the gap between rich and poor.'
Tom Wakeford, Brunel University (UK) and National Centre for Biological Sciences, India

'Despite surpluses, current global concentrations of food surpluses in some regions and deficits in others are unlikely to change soon.'
Patrick Webb, World Food Programme

Calories per person per day 1965-1995

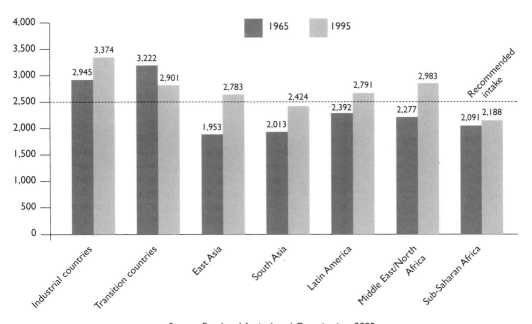

Source: Food and Agricultural Organization, 2000

Out-of-date machinery, such as this tractor in Albania, has contributed to declining food supplies in transition countries.

VIEWPOINT

'Unfortunately, future world food supplies may be less secure now than at any time in recent history.'
Lester Brown, Worldwatch Institute, 1999

FACT

Between 1970 and 1990 the area of HYV rice planted in developing countries increased from 30 to 74 per cent. Wheat increased from 20 to 70 per cent over the same period.

All regions, except the transition countries (Eastern Europe and the former Soviet Union), have increased their food supplies. In the transition states economic and political changes during the early 1990s caused dramatic decreases in production. In 1997 around 26 million, out of a total population of 413 million in these transition countries, were undernourished. East Asia, the Middle East and North Africa made the greatest improvements in food supply, while sub-Saharan Africa hardly progressed at all. It still has the lowest supplies of any region – below the 2,500 calories recommended as a daily minimum for an average adult. South Asia's supplies are also below this minimum, despite the impact of the Green Revolution in this area. In addition South Asia has the largest number of hungry people – 284 million, more than a third of the world total.

Food supply and population growth

South Asia and sub-Saharan Africa are also the regions where population growth is fastest. In South Asia population is growing at around 2.2 per cent per year, while in sub-Saharan Africa it is higher still at 2.8 per cent. (This compares with a world average of 1.6 per cent.) Many experts believe that food and population are closely linked and that food supplies will only improve when the birth rate slows down. Others suggest that hunger persists in these regions because of poverty rather than population growth. They often point to North Africa and the Middle East to support their case. Countries in these areas have been successful in increasing their food supplies, yet they have the fastest-growing populations in the world (up to 4.6 per cent per year in Saudi Arabia). They have succeeded in feeding their populations because of their stronger economies, many of them relying on oil. Their wealth allows them to import food if they suffer shortages, which many do because the climate is too dry to grow enough themselves. However, poorer economies in South Asia and sub-Saharan Africa cannot usually afford such imports without incurring debts that further add to their poverty.

VIEWPOINTS

'The overall lesson of the historical experience, which is probably also valid for the future, seems to be that the production system has so far had the capability of responding flexibly to meet increases in demand within reasonable limits.'
Food and Agricultural Organization, Italy, 2000

'It's true that we've kept up food production... but I have no doubt that some time in the next century food will be scarce.'
Paul Ehrlich, author of The Population Explosion, *1990*

These silos, used to store imported grain, are in Saudi Arabia.

DEBATE

What evidence can you find to suggest that we might be running out of food? Does it involve you personally? Thinking about the evidence you have found, do you think you should be concerned about population growth and food supplies?

FEEDING THE HUNGRY

VIEWPOINTS

'Cereal production in the developing world will not keep pace with demand, and net cereal imports by developing countries will almost double between 1995 and 2020 in order to fill the gap.'
Per Pinstrup-Anderson, International Food Policy Research Institute, USA

'The problem is that the poor do not have the income to buy food, whether or not it is available in local markets or in world markets.'
James Gustave Speth, United Nations Development Programme

FACT

In South Asia the gap between the production of grains and the demand for grains is expected to increase from 1 million tonnes in 1990 to 24 million tonnes by 2020.

Filling the gap

A country that cannot produce enough food for its own population has a food deficit (shortage). If it is to avoid problems of hunger, or even famine, then it must find food supplies from elsewhere. This is normally achieved by importing food from countries that have a surplus. We have seen, however, that some of the world's poorest countries can't afford such imports. This is especially so in years when global food supplies are scarcer than normal. In these years the lack of supplies means that countries compete with each other for what is available, the winner normally being the country that pays the highest price. Poor countries are particularly vulnerable in these circumstances because they have to pay even more to secure food for their people.

Changing world prices

A recent example of these price rises occurred in 1995. In that year wet weather in Canada and the USA, drought in sub-Saharan Africa and declining production in China and the former Soviet Union caused grain production to fall by 3.4 per cent compared with 1994. Even though this was a relatively small fall in yields it caused world grain prices to shoot up. As a result, wheat in 1995 was 18 per cent more expensive than in 1994 and 26 per cent more than in 1993. Fortunately, over the longer term, grain prices have fallen. In early 1999 they were at their lowest for twenty years, though they were starting to rise again by early 2001. The world price of grain will be increasingly important in the future because developing countries are expected to be unable to meet their own needs. Their imports of grain are therefore likely to increase from 109 million tonnes in 1995 to 195 million by 2020 and 274 million by 2030. Under such conditions, many of the poorest countries will become increasingly dependent on food aid to meet their needs.

Unforeseen natural events, such as this flooding of farmland by the Mississippi river in the USA, can damage crops and cause sudden changes in global food supplies and prices.

What is food aid?

You may have seen pictures on television or in newspapers of food being handed out to people in refugee camps. Many people think that this is what food aid is. They are right in a way, but only partly. In fact there are three main forms of food aid:

- **Emergency food aid** is normally given directly to people who are hungry as a result of droughts, natural disasters or conflicts.

- **Development food aid** is usually given to humanitarian groups (charities) who either distribute it to needy people or sell it to raise funds for development projects.

- **Economic food aid** is normally given to governments who distribute it or sell it on the world markets to raise money for other expenses or to pay off debts.

The food available for aid varies from year to year. It is mainly made up of developed countries' surpluses. Although developing countries also provide food aid, it is a small amount by comparison. In recent years the food available for aid has fallen by more than half, from 15 million tonnes in 1992 to 6.7 million tonnes in 1997. It is predicted to increase again to over 10 million tonnes in 2001, but aid agencies are warning that levels could be less reliable during the twenty-first century.

Emergency food aid

All types of food aid have been criticized, with the possible exception of emergency food aid. When people are threatened with starvation no one can really argue that they should not receive immediate assistance. However, even this form of aid has been criticized for the way in which food is distributed and the type of food that is given. Denmark is one country that has taken action on this. By changing from providing foods such as meat and cheese to peas, wheat and vegetable oil, Denmark has been able to donate six times more calories and three times more protein, and for less money.

Emergency food aid being flown into famine-struck Sudan as part of Operation Lifeline Sudan in 1994. Such food aid is only used when people are in danger of starvation.

VIEWPOINT

'Because of changes in agricultural policies...we are no longer in a situation of regular...agricultural surpluses. We can no longer assume surpluses will be available'
Edward Clay, Overseas Development Institute

Providing emergency food aid in conflict areas is particularly difficult. Roads are often blocked and fighting can mean that people are always moving, making them harder to reach. It can also be extremely dangerous for the aid workers. In some conflicts food aid is taken by the warring sides to feed their own fighters or even to sell so that they can buy more weapons. In these situations some people believe that food aid should be stopped because it helps support a war. But stopping could mean that thousands of innocent people starve – a very difficult decision.

Development food aid

Food aid for development is often sold to raise money to help improve people's standard of living in the long term. This might involve building wells to provide clean water, or helping local communities to set up their own businesses. In other situations food aid is given to people in return for them working on development projects such as building roads or schools. These are called 'food for work' programmes; in addition to providing food they can benefit local communities and teach new skills.

The International Committee of the Red Cross (ICRC) convoy heads towards Kabul, the capital of war-torn Afghanistan, taking food and medical supplies to people displaced by the conflict.

A food-for-work programme in Tigray Province, Ethiopia. Workers (including children) are given 6 kg of grain in return for 6 hours labour. Here they are helping to construct a dam.

Development food aid is also targeted at vulnerable groups such as pregnant women, young children, or the elderly to improve their health. For example, in South Africa a primary school nutrition programme provides food for over 5 million schoolchildren to help give them a healthier start in life.

All these schemes try to improve people's opportunities so that, if faced with food shortages in the future, they are better able to manage by themselves. Some argue that it would be better to provide money rather than food, because so much money ends up being used to pay the high cost of transporting the food around the world. These critics suggest that this money could pay for more development, but supporters of development food aid insist that it is an effective way of making sure food reaches the neediest people – something that cannot be guaranteed with donations of money.

VIEWPOINTS

'Hunger does not exist in isolation. It is both a cause and result of many other scourges that plague humanity, such as poverty, war, environmental degradation and discrimination.'
Food and Agricultural Organization, Italy

'Food relief can deflect attention from why there is food poverty; the feeling that the problem is being solved removes the pressure for action.'
Corinna Hawkes, Sustain (an alliance for better food and farming), UK

FACT

In 1999 about 12 million American children were hungry or at risk from hunger.

Economic food aid

Economic food aid (sometimes called 'budgetary food aid') is perhaps the most controversial. This is when governments sell food aid to earn money for other needs such as improving health or education. Unfortunately the money raised is not always spent in these ways. It has sometimes been used to buy weapons for the military or to improve the lives of the already rich and powerful. The money may also be used to try and pay off debts to other countries or international banks. Campaigners have argued that debts should be dropped to allow poor governments to spend the money on improving the lives of their own people. The UK government was one of the first to agree to this, but said it would only drop debts on condition that it received guarantees that the money saved would be spent on reducing poverty (including hunger). Although many agree with this so-called 'conditionality', some feel that governments should be free to choose how they spend their money and not be told by others.

Homeless people in Daytona Beach, Florida, USA, receive hot lunches as part of a local food aid scheme.

Some food experts believe economic food aid could be further improved if wealthy nations purchased food from developing countries with surpluses and then gave it to those with a deficit. In this way they would be promoting development in both surplus and deficit countries at the same time.

Different levels of food aid

Although most food aid is organized at a national level, it also occurs at a regional or local level. Even within individual communities, those with more food often assist those who are less fortunate. You may have done this yourself by donating tins or packets of food to charities helping the elderly or homeless in your community. It is important to realize that hunger can strike everywhere, not just in poor developing countries.

Self-reliance in food supplies can be helped by storing surpluses. This store in Burkina Faso is for millet.

Self-reliance

Food aid is currently needed to feed the hungry and is likely to become more important in the future. But experts consider that real success will only come when people or countries become self-reliant in food supplies. This is when they can either grow enough themselves or can afford to buy food from elsewhere to fill the gap. These experts tell us that self-reliance must be the aim in order to fight hunger in the long term – food aid is only a short-term solution.

DEBATE

Having learned more about feeding hungry people, what do you think is the best way forward and why? Under what conditions might you change your mind?

FOOD DISTRIBUTION

The global food trade

As we have seen, most people living in developed regions have enough food to eat, and in many cases perhaps too much. However, many of these developed countries cannot be described as self-sufficient in food because so much of their food is imported – sometimes from countries where people go hungry every day. You can see this for yourself next time you visit the supermarket. Look at where some of the food comes from and find the places on a map. This global food trade has grown enormously in recent years as consumer tastes have become more varied and technology has allowed us to distribute food more quickly around the globe. But who benefits from this?

Cultivating flower seeds in Sri Lanka (for export to Europe) instead of food for local consumption.

Cash cropping

Many of the food products we consume from developing countries are known as 'cash crops'. This simply means that farmers grow them to sell for money rather than for their own consumption (subsistence crops). In many areas farmers have converted their entire land to cash crops such as groundnuts, bananas, sugar, cocoa, coffee and tea.

More recently, crops such as tomatoes, chillies and mange-tout have been grown because they are highly valued in wealthy export markets (Europe and North America) where consumers demand fresh fruit and vegetables throughout the year.

In a good year farmers can earn large amounts from cash crops and for some countries they provide a major source of income. For example, around 70 per cent of Honduras' export earnings comes from bananas, while Uganda depends on coffee for a similar share of its income. However, there is also a risk with growing cash crops. World food prices change year by year, so farmers cannot be sure what price they will receive for their produce. For instance, in 1995 Uganda earned US$384 million from the sale of 169,000 tonnes of coffee, yet the previous year 194,000 tonnes was sold for just US$343 million – a difference of around US$500 per tonne in just one year. In this example Uganda benefited from better coffee prices, but it could just as easily turn the other way.

Tea cash crop in Tamil Nadu, India, using the most fertile land.

VIEWPOINTS

'...more than 90 per cent of the price paid by the consumer [for bananas] stays in the north and never reaches the producer. Most of the risks of producing a perishable fruit are, however, borne by the producer.'
New Internationalist magazine

'Why is it that producers of food are the first and most seriously affected by drought and famine and why do so few town dwellers die from hunger while rural areas are decimated by starvation and death?'
Amartya Sen, author of Poverty and Famines

FACT

80 per cent of all malnourished children in developing countries in the early 1990s lived in countries with surplus food.

VIEWPOINT

'If Third World nations had control over the food they produce, those countries would not suffer malnutrition nor death by hunger.'
Instituto del Tercer Mundo, Uruguay

Farmers are not only vulnerable to price changes. Cash crops are normally grown as a mono-crop (on their own) which means that they are more vulnerable to diseases, pests and environmental conditions. A disease outbreak or failed rains could destroy the whole crop, leaving farmers with nothing to feed their families. This risk became all too obvious to farmers in Honduras in October 1998 when Hurricane Mitch smashed through the country, killing around 6,000 people, making 2 million homeless, and destroying much of the country's valuable banana and coffee crops. It could take as long as ten years for farmers and the economy to recover fully.

Dependence on a single cash crop can be disastrous. In Honduras many banana plantations were completely destroyed by Hurricane Mitch in 1998, seriously affecting the country's economy.

You can't eat money!

Besides these risks, cash crops use land that could otherwise feed local people. For example, in Brazil an export cash crop of soya beans replaced black beans, which were an important low-cost food for millions of Brazil's poor. This ignorance of local food needs led to riots and the government was forced to import black beans from Chile to replace its own supplies.

The debate about the relative benefits of cash crops is very complex, but deciding whether or not to grow them is only part of the issue.

Food miles

With so much food being distributed throughout the world, some of it has travelled great distances by the time it reaches your shopping basket. While this may guarantee you fresh strawberries or peppers out of season, transporting foods over such large distances can harm the environment. For example, 1 tonne of bottled water travelling 1 km by road generates 2.4 g of carbon monoxide, 3.6 g of nitrogen oxides and 0.3 g of hydrocarbons.

Distributing food over such distances is also expensive, but because shops and importers do not want to lose customers they often pass this cost on by paying less to producers. Most coffee growers, for example, receive just 10 per cent of what we pay for their coffee in the supermarket, while most cocoa producers receive less than 4 per cent of the price of a chocolate bar.

VIEWPOINTS

'We need to improve the distribution of existing food supplies so that we don't have food surpluses in one part of the world and people starving in another part of the world.'
Elizabeth Dowdeswell, United Nations Environment Programme

'The world already produces enough to provide an adequate diet for everyone, if the food were distributed equitably. It is not.'
Food and Agricultural Organization, Italy

FACT

More than 33 per cent of apples and 80 per cent of pears eaten in northern Europe come from abroad. Some of them have travelled as far as 10,000 km!

Who receives what from banana cash cropping in Latin America?

Distribution and retail companies — 34%

Profit — 17%

15%

11%

International transport

Taxes

Import licences — 9%

5%

Producer — 5%

Export cost — 4%

Ripening

Source: UK Food Group 1999, 'Hungry for Power'

VIEWPOINTS

'A staggering amount of good food is landfilled each year, leading to environmental problems. Yet people on low incomes could be benefiting.'
Pete Riley, Friends of the Earth

'Food charity has never solved the problem of food poverty. It is a return to the medieval past, not a way forward...'
Tim Lang, Food Policy Centre, Thames Valley University, UK

Purchasing power

There is enormous competition between major supermarket chains to provide food at the lowest possible cost and attract more customers. In the UK this has become known as 'the supermarket war'. The lower prices might be good news for consumers, but surely someone has to pay for it? Several food experts are concerned that producers and environments in developing areas are suffering.

Large supermarkets are able to influence growers and governments because of their strong purchasing power. They can demand discounts because they buy in bulk, or insist that produce meets certain quality standards which may involve greater expense for the growers. Pressure to minimize costs may also mean less care for the environment as farmers cut corners or intensify production, using more chemicals and not allowing their land to lie fallow.

Many people argue for a return to local food supplies such as this farmer selling produce in Mississippi, USA.

One of the worst aspects of current food distribution is wastage. Supermarkets often buy more than they are able to sell and end up throwing a large amount away. In the UK about half a million tonnes of edible food is dumped in landfills every year at an estimated cost of £50 million. In the USA, 27 per cent of all food is thrown away, although the government assists firms in giving surpluses to charities that feed America's hungry. While this may be better than throwing food away, it does not solve the problem of people being hungry in the first place.

Supermarket waste in Hamburg, Germany.

A new food economy

Improving distribution to give growers a better deal and reduce waste will, it is argued, only be possible if there is a new food economy. More food will need to be grown locally, reducing transportation and storage costs. Growers must be paid a fair price for their produce that allows them to sustain their family and conserve their environment – consumers must be prepared to pay for this. Changes are happening. For example, Fair Trade products in Britain and TransFair products in the USA, such as coffee, tea, chocolate and bananas, are now available in many supermarkets. People are more interested in where their food comes from and what its real cost is. That must be a good start.

FACT

The UK supermarket chain Sainsbury's reduced food wastage from 23 per cent to 10 per cent between 1994 and 2000.

VIEWPOINTS

'...most importantly, people are asking questions about the food they eat rather than just blindly consuming what is given them.'
John Brunton, Geographical Magazine, UK

'Consumers want to understand the way food is produced. Over the last 45 years our link with the land was severed. We are re-establishing that link.'
Rob Haward, Soil Association, UK

DEBATE

Discuss with your friends and family how your diet might change if food was not distributed from around the world to your local supermarket. What foods would be available from your own country?

HEALTH AND NUTRITION

Quality matters

Consuming the right number of calories is not enough. It is also important that we eat the right type of foods and in the right amounts – a balanced diet. Scientists who study our diets and their nutrient content are called dieticians and nutritionists. They study the foods we eat and analyse how they benefit or harm us. We know, for example, that too much fat in our diets can make us overweight and cause illnesses such as heart disease or diabetes. Too little of certain nutrients can also cause problems. A lack of vitamin A, for instance, kills around 2 million children annually. A further 350,000 go blind each year because their diet lacks this important vitamin found in foods such as milk, egg yolks, fish and vegetables (especially carrots). It is very important when thinking about food supplies to consider not just the quantity of food available, but also its quality. If the food you eat does not match your body's needs then you become malnourished. So malnourishment is not always due to having too little food. More often, it is caused by poor diet.

Young people eating burgers, one of the most popular types of fast food.

Less active lifestyles are leading to health problems.

VIEWPOINTS

'As people change their diets from being vegetable based to being animal fat based, the problem of obesity worsens.'
Professor Chunming Chen, Chinese Academy of Preventative Medicine

'...we resemble a lion or a bird of prey which, once it has gorged on its kill, will hardly move until hunger forces it to chase prey again. Except that all we need to do is waddle to the fridge.'
Simon Jones, Green Futures magazine

Poor diets

Many people in the world have a poor diet and not just in poor countries. In fact, diets in the wealthiest countries are becoming worse every year as people eat more and more junk food such as burgers, pizzas, crisps and sweets. These are high-fat or high-sugar foods and, combined with less active lifestyles, they are responsible for a growing obesity problem in much of Europe and North America. In the USA 55 per cent of adults (almost 100 million people) are overweight, while in the UK and Canada the proportion of obese (severely overweight) people has more than doubled since 1990. This problem is becoming particularly noticeable in children who have grown up eating such foods. Many also spend much of their leisure time using computers or watching television instead of engaging in more physical activities such as sports. In the USA and UK some parents have become so worried about their children's health that they have sent them on special 'fat camps' to help them lose weight.

FACT

Over 75 per cent of the food eaten in the USA is processed in some way. This costs around US$10 billion per year – 70 per cent more than it costs to grow.

VIEWPOINTS

'If the rest of Asia, including China, changes its dietary patterns so that they are similar to those of Japan, this will put enormous pressure on the future food supplies of Asian countries.'
Lester Brown, Worldwatch Institute

'Children have been eating less, but are watching more TV – which includes videos, Playstations or PC screens.'
Dr John Reilly, Glasgow University

FACT

Over 40 per cent of child blindness each year is caused by a lack of vitamin A in the diet. This could be avoided by a simple vitamin supplement treatment costing just 4p (US$0.06) per child per year.

FACT

1 gram of proteins or carbohydrate contains 4 calories, but 1 gram of fat contains 9 calories.

Eating more meat

One of the most notable dietary trends is the increasing amount of meat that is consumed as countries develop. Meat is an important source of proteins that build and renew body tissue, but it also contains animal fats, too much of which can lead to obesity and other health problems. The amount of meat consumed per person more than doubled in the last fifty years of the twentieth century. Today we each eat about 37 kg of meat per year, though this varies from just 6 kg per person in South Asia to almost 80 kg each (the weight of an average adult) in developed countries. Meat consumption is growing fastest in Asia and Latin America, where increased wealth means that people's diets are becoming more westernized. In Japan, for example, meat consumption increased by 360 per cent between the early 1960s and early 1990s. Meat consumption is lowest and slowest-growing in the poorest countries of sub-Saharan Africa and South Asia.

Besides health concerns, increased meat consumption has been blamed for causing greater hunger because supplies of cereals are used to feed animals instead of people. In beef production 10 calories of feed are needed to produce just 1 calorie worth of meat. On a global scale, about 36 per cent of world cereals are used in animal feed, though in developed countries this is over 70 per cent. Despite these figures, agricultural scientists say there is no clear evidence that human beings are hungry because of cereals being used to feed animals instead of people.

Nutrition deficiencies

In many of the poorest countries people lack the basic nutrients required for a healthy life. Nutrient deficiencies can lead to various diseases such as kwashiorkor (protein deficiency), beri-beri (vitamin B1 deficiency) and rickets (vitamin D deficiency) that weaken the body's immune system. People are more likely to fall ill, especially children who are more vulnerable to diseases. In developing countries a child under five dies every 4.7 seconds of causes related to nutrient deficiencies – that's about 18,300 children every day or four in the time it has taken you to read this sentence.

FACT

Illness related to obesity has been estimated to account for up to 7 per cent of developed countries' health budgets.

The world's appetite for fast food burgers has led to large areas of the Amazon forest being cleared for cattle ranches to raise beef cows.

Young children are especially at risk from nutrient deficiencies. Regular checks at health centres like this one in Angahna, Mexico, help to spot such problems early on.

VIEWPOINTS

'We know that nutrition in the womb and in the first two years of life is important all through that person's life.'
Dianne Spearman, World Food Programme

'The agricultural revolution must take into account that half of humanity is women.'
Speciosa Wandira Kazibwe, Vice-President of Uganda

Nutrient deficiency in children is assessed by measuring their weight compared to their height. This allows doctors to see whether they are growing normally for their age or whether they might be malnourished. In developed countries fewer than 1 per cent of children under five suffer from major deficiencies, but in South Asia 51 per cent are underweight and 52 per cent suffer from stunted growth. For many of these children their problems start at birth. If pregnant women do not receive a balanced diet their babies may be born weak and underweight. In South Asia, a third of all new babies are of a low birth-weight (less than 2.5 kg) and in Bangladesh this rises to 50 per cent. How does this compare with what you weighed when you were born?

The main cause of nutrient deficiency is poverty. Many deficiencies can be overcome by giving cheap supplements (such as vitamin A capsules needed for healthy eyesight) when children are taken to clinics to be immunized. However, some of the poorest countries can't afford immunization programmes and basic supplements that could save millions of lives every year. Deficiencies can also be tackled by adding important nutrients to people's normal diet. Iodine is one such nutrient, important for a healthy brain. By adding iodine to salt during production, the mental retardation of an estimated 12 million children has been prevented.

Education and improved nutrition

Long-term solutions will require permanent improvements in nutrition, and education is the key to this. People (and especially women) who understand the benefits of a healthy diet will not only improve their own, but also pass their knowledge on to future generations. Between 1970 and 1995 women's education was responsible for 43 per cent of the decline in the number of malnourished children from 204 million to 167 million. In Uganda nurses visit rural villages to teach women about better childhood nutrition by holding practical demonstrations. The women complain, however, that the men often decide what is planted and how much to spend on buying additional foods. This makes it hard to put what they have learned into practice.

> **FACT**
>
> **At least £166 million (US$250 million) is spent on slimming aids in the UK each year.**

This poster in Ibadan, Nigeria, is encouraging mothers to breastfeed their children. Breast milk is rich in nutrients and helps protect babies from childhood diseases.

VIEWPOINTS

'The effects of childhood malnutrition last a lifetime, and even into succeeding generations.'
Marc Cohen and Don Reeves, Bread for the World Institute, USA

'...while the health-and-environment-conscious middle class may exalt the virtues of lentils and organic bean sprouts, poorer communities simply don't have much access to fresh, affordable and wholesome food.'
Simon Jones, Green Futures magazine, UK

Education and nutrition programmes are also necessary in developed countries. The consumption of fresh fruit and vegetables in the USA fell by a third during the last century and similar declines have been seen in parts of Europe. Governments are now trying to reverse such trends to improve the health of their populations. In the UK, for example, a scheme was introduced in 2000 to encourage schoolchildren to eat more fruit; each child is given one piece of free fruit every day. If the scheme is successful it will be expanded across the whole country.

Another improvement in most developed countries has been an increase in the information about nutritional content printed on food packaging. This information enables consumers to consider, for example, the fat content of a product or its contribution of certain vitamins to their recommended daily allowance (RDA). Such information is only useful if people look at it, however. Have a look at the food packaging in your home and see what it tells you about the food you are eating.

A healthier future

Globally, people are undoubtedly healthier today than at any time in the past, but there are still considerable problems in both developed and developing countries. In developed countries, high-fat and high-sugar diets are costing health systems billions of dollars to treat the resulting heart disease, strokes, cancers and other illnesses. By contrast, the number of malnourished children in sub-Saharan Africa increased from 18.5 million in 1970 to 31.4 million in 1995 and there are expected to be as many as 55 million by 2020. South Asia will remain the area in worst health, however, with well over a third of its children still underweight in 2020. In 1996 world leaders from 186 countries gathered at the World Food Summit in Rome and pledged to cut malnutrition to half its 1990-92 level by 2015. In the year 2001 this target looked unlikely to be met but, even if it is, it will still leave 400 million malnourished people in the world. Many more may have enough calories, but continue to suffer from life-threatening nutrient deficiencies.

A malnourished boy collects grain left over from an air drop by the World Food Programme in southern Sudan. At the 1996 World Food Summit, leaders agreed to halve such severe malnutrition by 2015.

DEBATE

Make a list of the food you eat over a day or week. Looking at your list, think about what you could do to improve the nutritional content of your diet. What are the benefits of eating a balanced diet?

IMPROVING FOOD SUPPLIES

VIEWPOINT

'The fact that per capita [per person] food production has been flat or possibly falling for a decade is terrifying. Any future increases in food production must come from technology and research, not new land.'
Jessica Matthews. Council on Foreign Relations. USA

High-tech intensive farming, as in this lettuce factory in Germany, is one approach to improving food supplies.

The next revolution?

The dramatic increase in food supplies since the 'Green Revolution' of the 1970s has shown some evidence of slowing down during the 1990s, sparking new fears of food shortages. There are now fewer reserves and less cultivated land per person than in the early 1970s when the food crisis first struck. In this same period the world population increased by 2.36 billion and may increase by that number again by 2035. So is there real cause for concern?

Agricultural scientists tell us that new technologies in farming and food production will provide plentiful supplies in the future. Sceptics, however, argue that these technologies will harm the environment and involve using dangerous and untested ideas. They argue that it would be better to control population, reduce food wastage and return to more natural food production methods instead. It is not entirely clear what the next food supply revolution will be, or where it will take place. But food supplies must improve over the next few decades, and there are several ways in which this could be achieved.

Biotechnology

Because scientists now understand more about the natural world than at any time in history, they are able to manipulate nature using biotechnology. One of the main uses of biotechnology is genetic engineering to improve food supplies. Such foods are known as genetically modified (GM) foods because they are produced by modifying (changing) the genes of plants or animals. Genes are the biological

This scientist is researching genetically modified tomato plants grown in the USA.

codes contained within the cells of every living thing that determine the way they look and grow. In humans they determine all our characteristics, from how tall we will be, to the colour of our hair and eyes. By changing the genes of plants it is possible to make them produce higher yields, resist pests and diseases, improve their nutritional value and even become more drought-resistant. The benefits could be enormous, not only for increasing food supplies but also for protecting the environment and improving health and nutrition.

FACT

High Yield Varieties (HYVs) helped world grain output increase by 170 per cent between 1950 and 1992 from just a 1 per cent increase in cropland.

Protesters in the UK destroy a field of GM rape seed oil. They are concerned about the safety of GM crops for people and the environment.

VIEWPOINT

'Strong opposition to genetically modified food (GM food) in the European Union has resulted in severe restrictions for modern biotechnology for agriculture.'
International Food Policy Research Institute, World Food Prospects 1999

However, some people believe that GM foods pose considerable risks to human health and the environment. So far, there is little evidence to support such claims, but anti-GM campaigners have been very successful in raising public concern through demonstrations and media reports. In parts of Europe public concern is so strong that supermarkets and restaurants now advertise that their products are GM-free in order to avoid losing business. So is there any basis to these fears? Surely improving food supplies can only be beneficial?

Tampering with nature

Campaigners argue that GM technology is dangerous because it is tampering with nature and too new for us to know the possible long-term effects. Some governments have accepted this and are conducting field trials of the new crops to assess the risks. But campaigners say that even these should not be allowed because pollen or seed from the new GM crops may escape and threaten natural biodiversity. This happened in 1998 in Lincolnshire in the UK when pollen from a GM rape seed oil trial contaminated normal rape seed in a nearby field. The rape seed was destroyed and the company responsible was prosecuted by the UK government. Despite this incident, the UK government is continuing with GM trials. But protests have continued too. In 1999 Greenpeace campaigners publicly destroyed and uprooted several GM field trials of maize.

Power and control

Perhaps most worrying is the power and control that the companies producing GM seeds could have. These companies are multi-billion dollar corporations that might have the ability to influence government policy on agriculture, the environment and even consumer safety. Anti-GM campaigners are concerned that these corporations could become so powerful that they might actually harm food security (availability) rather than improve it. One company is among the main causes of concern because of its proposal to introduce so-called 'terminator technology'. This is built into GM seeds so that they can only be used for one growing season and not saved for replanting. The company says this policy ensures the highest yields for farmers, but critics say it just means they can increase their profits by charging farmers for new seed every year.

VIEWPOINTS

'Leading Africans have made it clear that the technology will not help food security on the continent.'
John Madeley, author specializing in food supply issues

'In Africa GM food could almost literally weed out poverty. Europeans tell us it is too dangerous. They tell us "Africa, this is not for you. Keep off." You in Europe are entitled to your own opinion. But I think it is dangerous when you tell everyone else what to do.'
Florence Wambugu, International Service for the Acquisition of Agri-biotech Applications

The main problem is the poor farmers who use these seeds to produce between 15 and 20 per cent of the world's current food supply – enough to feed 1.4 billion people. If they cannot afford to buy new seed each year how many millions of people may go hungry?

A GM future?

So what place are GM foods likely to hold in future food supply? These companies claim that using biotechnology is the only way we will manage to feed the growing human population. Many scientists agree that biotechnology will have to play an increasingly important role and the global area cultivated with GM crops has already increased – from 1.7 million hectares in 1996 to almost 28 million hectares by 1998. However the uptake of GM crops is not yet global. The USA accounted for 74 per cent of the GM crop area in 1998, with Argentina and Canada making up a further 25 per cent. Hardly any GM crops have been planted in Europe or in developing countries that could potentially benefit from them most. Until governments and consumers are convinced that GM foods are safe, uptake will be limited. So alternative methods of improving food supplies must be explored.

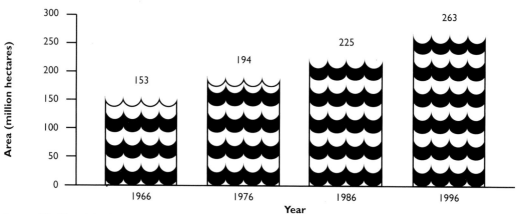

Global area of irrigated crops 1966-96

Source: Worldwatch Institute

Irrigation

Irrigation has been used by humankind for thousands of years. In Egypt it is still possible to see systems being used today that were first used during the time of the pharaohs. Many experts believe that water will be the main factor in determining future world food supplies. Globally, around 70 per cent of water is used for agriculture, but demands are increasing for water for industrial and domestic uses. Many of the world's poorest countries also happen to be in regions where water supplies are extremely unreliable and irrigation may be the only way to guarantee food supplies. Globally, irrigated land is said to have been responsible for over half the increase in food supplies between the mid-1960s and mid-1980s. Today about 40 per cent of the world's food comes from the 17 per cent of cropland that is irrigated.

VIEWPOINTS

'Biotech foods are new, they are different, and they deserve special regulations. The industry should drop its opposition to tougher regulations. That could boost consumer confidence and disarm the critics.'
Paul Raeburn, Business Week

'Labelling is the key issue. If you put a label on genetically engineered food you might as well put a skull and crossbones on it.'
Spokesperson for Asgrow Seed Company

FACT

If the USA reduced the amount of food it wasted each day by a third it could feed an additional 26 million people – a population equivalent to famine-struck North Korea in 2000.

Traditional types of irrigation, such as this donkey-powered system in Egypt, have existed for hundreds of years, but they are often wasteful of scarce water resources.

FACT

To meet the demands of predicted crop expansion, global irrigation may need to increase by over 300 per cent – an amount of water equal to twenty-four times the annual flow of the Nile, the world's longest river!

Irrigation has its problems, however. It normally involves the construction of expensive dams for storing river or rain water and channels or pipes to carry this to the fields. Because of the expense, much irrigated land is used to grow cash crops for export to recover costs. In such situations irrigation does little to improve local food supplies. Many of the techniques currently used also waste large quantities of water. Surface irrigation, where water is allowed to flood onto the land, wastes up to 60 per cent of water compared to sprinkler irrigation which wastes around 30 per cent. This wastage can cause environmental problems such as over-extraction and water-logging.

In many areas irrigation also leads to higher levels of diseases associated with water, such as diarrhoea, malaria and bilharzia. As well as causing direct illness, these diseases weaken people so that they are unable to farm their land efficiently and their yields fall.

Sprinkler irrigation, here in County Durham, UK, often uses more water than is necessary. This can result in water-logging and salinization, especially in warmer climates.

Drip irrigation

Improved techniques such as drip irrigation waste less than 10 per cent of the water used and because the water is supplied drip by drip, directly to the roots, the other side-effects are also reduced. It is extremely expensive though, and requires expert knowledge and computer-controlled equipment. Israel is the world leader in drip irrigation and is involved in training others, such as companies in Kenya, who use it to grow high-quality flowers and vegetables for export to Europe. The use of such technology to produce local food supplies is at present too expensive for most countries to consider.

Turning to fish

Biotechnology and irrigation are both methods of improving food supplies that focus on intensification – producing more of the same food on the same land. The alternative to this is diversification, where food supplies are increased by finding new or alternative food sources. One of the main forms of diversification has been the increase in fishing around the world. In 1950 the world fish catch was 19 million tonnes, but this increased by almost 500 per cent to 96 million tonnes by 1997. This worldwide increase in fishing has been referred to as the 'Blue Revolution'.

Fish like these just harvested from the sea by Goa, India, are becoming increasingly important in meeting global food demands.

VIEWPOINT

'...irrigation development has in some places become ultimately self-destructive. All too often the short-term gain in production, leading to intensive settlement, was followed by long-term loss in the form of water resource depletion and pollution, as well as soil erosion and degradation.'
Dr Daniel Hillel, environmental scientist and hydrologist, USA

Fishing for herring off Ruegen Island, Germany; the growth in large-scale commercial fishing threatens fish stocks and traditional fisheries.

The increase in fishing has contributed significantly to food supplies and provides an important source of protein and vitamins. However, there is concern that fish stocks are being depleted too rapidly. Sophisticated equipment allows fishing fleets to track fish more efficiently and modern drift nets, spanning up to 40 km, mean that very few fish escape.

VIEWPOINTS

'The over-exploitation of fish stocks is a threat to world food security. Another problem I see is when fish become a crop and a product for the market rather than something that poor people collect in the wild for their subsistence.'
Dr Sten Sverdrup-Jensen, Institute for Fisheries Management and Coastal Community Development, Denmark

'To meet the future demand for fish, the world will have to rely far, far less on natural stocks from the open oceans and more on aquaculture.'
Meryl Williams, International Centre for Living Aquatic Resources Management, Philippines

Inland fisheries have also grown dramatically, such as Lake Victoria in East Africa. Between 1979 and 1989 the fish catch there increased from about 100,000 tonnes to 500,000 and the number of fishermen nearly trebled. Most noticeable, however, was the increase in the catch of Nile Perch – a species introduced to the lake in the 1950s. In 1979 just 1,000 tonnes were caught, but by 1989 this had exploded to 325,000 tonnes. During the 1990s Lake Victoria's fisheries, like those around the world, have suffered from over-fishing and fish caught there today are smaller and less plentiful than in the past.

Growth in the global fishing industry has also meant more commercial fishing in waters previously used by local communities. In many areas this important source of food has been reduced or destroyed by commercial fishing for the more profitable urban or export markets. A complex system of quotas (limits) has been introduced in many of the world's fisheries in an attempt to conserve and replace stocks. In reality it is often difficult to control fishing activities and illegal fishing continues to threaten remaining stocks.

Aquaculture

One method of preserving stocks has been the development of fish farming (or aquaculture). Today almost a third of the world's fish supply comes from such sources, with Thailand, Canada and Scandinavia among the main producers. However, aquaculture has had problems with disease outbreaks killing entire stocks, and escaping fish and waste pollution damaging local environments. For example, off Vancouver Island in Canada, farmed salmon are now regularly caught by fleets fishing for wild salmon. And in western Scotland pollution and diseases from salmon farms have been blamed for the collapse of the local population of wild salmon. Nevertheless, supporters of aquaculture remind us that it is a relatively new form of farming and that, despite early problems, it will become increasingly important in the coming decades.

Fish farms in Hardanger Fjord, Norway.

FACT

In February 2000 the New Zealand King Salmon Company was forced to destroy its GM fish after photos showing their deformed heads caused public concerns about safety.

VIEWPOINTS

'When faced with resource shortages, many people automatically look to the sea as a limitless supplier of food.'
Tim Flannery, scientist, and author of The Future Eaters

'Current trends in the price of fish cast doubt on how much longer this important food will be widely available to the world's poor.'
Population Action International, 'People in the Balance'

DEBATE

Think about the different approaches to increasing food supplies and decide whether you think it is best to intensify production or diversify supplies. What are your reasons?

FOOD SUPPLY AND THE ENVIRONMENT

Starving the earth

In the past people farmed the land to meet their own needs, and human impact on the environment was relatively small. The lack of machinery and chemical fertilizers meant that the natural environment limited what people could grow. If the soil showed signs of losing its fertility it would be left to recover (or 'lie fallow') and a new

Forest clearance for agriculture has caused water tables in Western Australia to rise, because trees are no longer there to use water stored in the soils. As the water builds up, it brings mineral salts from deep underground, leading to salinization over a wide area.

field would be dug nearby. Similarly, nomadic peoples, such as the Tuareg of West Africa, would regularly move their animals (cattle, goats or camels) to fresh pastures and water-holes to allow the environment to recover. Such processes allowed people to live within the limits of their environment or what is often referred to as its 'carrying capacity' – the population an environment can sustainably support.

As human numbers have grown, however, we have placed increasing pressure on our environment's ability to support us. Science and technology have given us machinery to farm ever larger areas, and chemicals to increase plant yields. But can such intensification continue and at what cost? This question is especially important, given that there is no longer always room to simply move to new ground when food supplies run short or the environment begins to suffer. Many environmental experts believe we have already exceeded our planet's carrying capacity and that food supplies are unsustainable. They have warned that we are in grave danger of starving the earth we depend on.

Water damage

We have seen how important irrigation has been in improving food supplies, but it can also have a downside for the environment. If too much water is applied to fields it can result in water-logging or salinization. Water-logging occurs when water is applied faster than the soil is able to absorb it. If the plants' roots sit in water then growth is reduced. Over longer periods, continued over-application can raise the water table and damage vast areas of land. The water table in the Indus Valley, Pakistan, was 30 m below ground before irrigation was introduced in the middle of the last century, but within years it rose to within a few centimetres of the surface in low-lying areas.

VIEWPOINTS

'There is little cropland remaining that can easily be brought under production and there is little additional irrigation capacity that can be easily developed'
Lester Brown, Worldwatch Institute

'It is estimated that the world has 1.5 billion hectares of land fit for agriculture. However, less than half are used to produce food.'
Instituto del Tercer Mundo, Uruguay, 'The World Guide' 1999

FACT

It takes 1,000 tonnes of water to produce just 1 tonne of grain.

VIEWPOINT

'If soil and water are healthy, the ecosystem has an opportunity to remain healthy. If soil and water are unhealthy or deteriorating in quality, the system is probably unsustainable.'
US Department of Agriculture

FACT

The water table beneath the northern plain, which produces around 40 per cent of China's grain harvest, is falling by as much as 1.5 m per year due to over-extraction.

VIEWPOINT

'If you look down on the Punjab [in India] from an aircraft, you will see...patches of grey decay. This is salinization, a rotting of the land [that] erupts unpredictably in disconnected patches...nibbling away at the welfare of the Punjab.'

L. Cantor, author of A world Geography of Irrigation

Salinization occurs as water evaporates, leaving high concentrations of mineral salts in the soil. This problem is made worse by the use of fertilizers that further increase the salinity of soils if not carefully controlled. Like water-logging, salinization is a result of over-watering and is particularly problematic in hotter climates due to high rates of evaporation. Globally, it is estimated that between 10 and 24 per cent of irrigated land suffers reduced crop yields due to salinization. In the worst-affected countries (such as India, Pakistan, Iraq and Egypt) up to half of all irrigated land suffers from salinization or water-logging, severely threatening present and future crop production.

More developed countries also suffer, with Australia, the USA and parts of the former Soviet Union being particularly affected. Up to 35 per cent of the USA's irrigated land has salinity problems and large areas of farmland have become unproductive. In Montana, USA, about 32,000 hectares of farmland were unusable in 1971 and by 1987 this had risen to around 121,000 hectares – almost 2 per cent of Montana's total crop area.

Salinization and water-logging also damage non-irrigated land by changing the hydrological systems in the local area. In several countries areas of cropland have become unproductive following rises in the water table from nearby irrigated schemes. In coastal areas salinization can result from the over-extraction of groundwater and falling water tables. As water is pumped from natural underground reservoirs (aquifers), salt water from the sea or ocean can seep through the ground and turn the aquifers saline. (This has happened in California, USA, and Oman in the Middle East.) In such conditions, even the most careful irrigation management can lead to problems of salinity.

Over-extraction can also affect downstream environments, as famously demonstrated by the Aral Sea in Central Asia – among the world's greatest environmental disasters. Rapid expansion of irrigated cotton crops in Kazakhstan and Uzbekistan required water to be extracted from the two rivers feeding the Aral Sea, reducing their flow by almost 90 per cent between 1981 and 1990. Once the world's fourth largest inland water body (67,000 km² in the 1950s), the Aral Sea is today 55 per cent smaller. Its shores are now almost 100 km from the fishing villages it once supported. Fish are dying as salts accumulate in the shrinking waters, reducing the annual catch from 44,000 tonnes in the 1950s to nothing, with some 60,000 job losses as a result.

FACT

Crop losses due to salinization in the Colorado Basin in the USA could reach an annual value of US$270 million by 2010.

The rapid reduction in the waters of the Aral Sea, here in Kazakhstan, has become a global example of the dangers of large-scale irrigation schemes.

Water management

Salinization and water-logging can be avoided by improving water management. Lining irrigation channels to prevent leaks, and educating farmers about the water needs of their crops to avoid over-watering, are both effective measures. Leaving irrigated land fallow at times also reduces problems by allowing water time to drain, flushing salts away with it. However, most irrigated land is used for intensive export agriculture (often not even for food, as in the Sudan where it is used to grow cotton). Leaving it fallow may mean a loss of income. But this loss is normally small compared to the cost of recovering salinized or water-logged land, if it is ever possible to recover it.

'Silent Spring'

In 1962 Rachel Carson alerted the world to the potential hazards of agrochemicals (fertilizers, pesticides and herbicides) used in modern farming to our health and environment. Her book *Silent Spring* described how the birds that once marked the return of spring in the agricultural lands of America could no longer be heard. Not because they had gone anywhere, but because they were dying.

Chemicals (especially pesticides) used to increase food supplies were shown to affect the local environment dramatically. Pesticides were destroying the food of birds and small mammals, causing major crashes in their populations and even localized extinctions. Even those that survived were often poisoned by residues entering the food chain. Over time these led to deformities that further threatened species survival. For example, research in Canada and the USA showed many birds being born with crossed bills or missing eyes, and in some animal species males were failing to reach maturity and breed successfully. Despite such evidence, the use of agrochemicals continues

Pesticides can cause damage, but without them many argue that food supplies would decline.

to increase, with global sales rising from virtually nothing in the 1940s to an industry with sales of US$31 billion in 1998. So why are they used?

In the fight to improve food supplies they were considered by many to play a vital role in eliminating the estimated 10,000 insect species, 30,000 weeds and other diseases and pests that annually cause up to 40 per cent of global crops to be lost. If these losses could be reduced (or eliminated) it would have a huge impact on food supplies.

However, many environmentalists now believe that agrochemicals have brought few benefits and may even have made things worse. Pesticide use, which increased more than eleven-fold between 1940 and

FACT

In North Africa in 1988 a swarm of locusts was measured at 120 km by 26 km. It contained an estimated 150 billion insects destroying 300,000 tonnes of vegetation per day.

FACT

The World Health Organization estimates that 3 million people are poisoned, and 200,000 are killed, by using pesticides each year.

Locusts are a serious threat to food supplies in some parts of the world, such as here in Mauritania, West Africa. Chemicals can help control such pests, but pesticide resistance is becoming a problem.

2000, is particularly worrying. In addition to killing the pests they were designed to kill, these chemicals have often wiped out species of great importance to food supplies such as butterflies and bees which help pollinate crops. Pests are increasingly becoming resistant to pesticides too. Some estimates suggest that crop losses due to insect pests have doubled since 1960, with over 1,600 insects now pesticide-resistant. Farmers and chemical companies have responded by developing more powerful pesticides and applying greater quantities, but this often just encourages greater resistance. In the USA, for example, despite an increase in pesticide use of over 1,000 per cent between 1940 and 1990, crop losses due to insects rose from 30 to 37 per cent.

Modern intensive agriculture uses large quantities of chemical fertilizers to compensate for the fact that farmers cannot afford to let land lie fallow. But pumping fertilizers onto the soil causes problems. At least half the fertilizer usually escapes into the environment where it can enter the water cycle, contaminating drinking water and causing eutrophication (where a build-up of fertilizers in the water encourages rapid plant and algae growth). Over time this increased plant growth robs the water of oxygen and begins to affect other aquatic life. Algal blooms are an obvious sign of eutrophication. In extreme cases this can lead to the death of all local fish.

Back to nature

Some farmers, consumers and governments now believe that the continued use of chemicals is unsafe and are instead promoting more natural farming methods. One example is the organic movement, which is growing rapidly in many parts of the world as consumers start to demand healthier food. However, millions of poor farmers in developing areas, who practise virtually organic farming, also suffer from regular crop failures and hunger. What is needed is better knowledge and practice to simultaneously boost food production and protect the environment.

VIEWPOINTS

'As much as novel biotechnology may attempt to improve breeds, it is not possible to replace lost diversity. Loss of diversity is forever.'
Keith Hammond, Food and Agricultural Organization, Italy

'In organic farming you are using the land to its capabilities, rather than artificially pumping it beyond them. At any one time 25 per cent or more of the land has to be grass or clover to "fix" nitrogen into the soil.'
Rob Haward, Soil Association, UK

Percentage of European farmland organically farmed in 2000

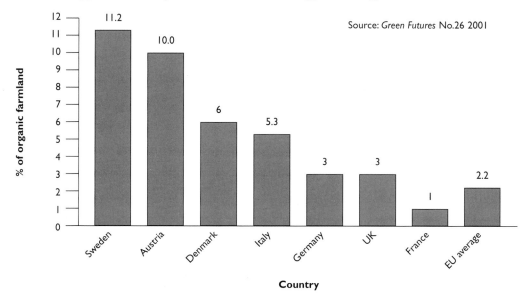

Source: *Green Futures* No.26 2001

Agroecology (an environment-friendly approach to food production) is likely to be increasingly important in the future. It works by copying natural ecosystems, such as forests or wetlands, so that the different parts support and sustain each other. For example, plants known as 'legumes' (beans, peas, etc) are able to capture nitrogen from the environment and fix it in the soil. By planting leguminous crops with normal crops (intercropping) or by alternating plantings (rotational cropping), the need for damaging and expensive nitrate fertilizers can be reduced or even eliminated. Allowing animals to graze the remnants of harvested fields is another agroecology practice found throughout much of sub-Saharan Africa, for example. It provides livestock with extra food and their faeces provide rich natural fertilizer for the next growing season.

Improved techniques such as contour ploughing can also increase food supplies. Sloping land is ploughed following the contours, so reducing run-off of water and subsequent soil erosion. On steeper slopes, terracing or bunds (ridges) can be added to further conserve soil and water. In Honduras, Central America, an agroecology system using a mixture of contour ploughing, bunds, intercropping with legumes and fertilizing with chicken manure, led to grain yields rising from 400 kg per hectare to 1,600 kg in just a few seasons. Not only were yields higher, but the costs of production fell dramatically.

Intercropping, as with these bananas and cabbages in Vinales, Cuba, copies natural ecosystems and reduces the need for the artificial chemical inputs used in mono-cropping.

An introduced weevil has eaten most of the choking water hyacinth that used to cover large parts of Lake Victoria in Uganda, disrupting fishing.

Agroecology also has new answers to the problem of pests. Integrated Pest Management (IPM) uses natural enemies to attack weeds and pests instead of chemicals. In Lake Victoria, for instance, a weevil has been introduced that feeds on the water hyacinth plant (a weed that had covered large areas of the lake, killing fish, disrupting transport and blocking the Owen Falls hydroelectric dam in Jinja, Uganda). In Indonesia pesticide use has fallen by 60 per cent since the introduction of IPM programmes in 1986 and rice yields have grown by a quarter.

Although such systems may sometimes produce lower yields than intensive modern farming methods, their supporters claim they produce healthier food that is safer for the environment. The low set-up costs mean that poorer farmers benefit and in the longer term they are more sustainable than intensive farming practices.

FACT

In Europe the number of common birds (such as the skylark, turtle dove and tree sparrow) has fallen by 60 per cent or more since 1970 due mainly to intensive chemical agriculture.

DEBATE

Those concerned about the environment have sometimes been blamed for preventing further reductions in hunger. Do you think this is a fair accusation? Or do you think they are right to be concerned? Why?

AN END TO HUNGER?

Feeding tomorrow's children

It appears that the world has enough food to feed future generations, but whether this will become a reality or not is less certain. Can the environment sustain increases in food production when it is already showing signs of damage? And will those who currently have least access to food supplies become food secure as a result of fairer distribution? To a large extent this will depend on the actions of governments, but you and I can also play a part through our own actions.

Government support

Greater investment by governments could increase food supplies dramatically. This could be done directly, for instance by providing farmers with

This Food and Agricultural Organization workshop in Bolivia is helping to educate farmers about improvements in farming methods. Sharing knowledge is considered central to improving food supplies.

improved seeds or livestock, or indirectly by promoting education and providing better information for farmers. In developing countries, rural communities, who produce much of the world's food, are often very poorly educated. Extending their basic education would enable them to read instructions, for example on chemical packets. This would ensure the correct use of agricultural chemicals, reducing the environmental and health problems associated with over-application. Educated farmers are also able to keep records of previous harvests and to better predict food shortages before it is too late. In East Africa, for example, educated farmers are able to take advantage of government support schemes, but those who cannot read or write the necessary forms are often left out.

Many experts believe agriculture must be given greater importance. Governments tend to focus on industry and commerce because they appear more valuable, but the neglect of farming could prove very expensive if food supplies begin to run out. Commercial companies are investing millions of dollars in improving food supplies through the use of biotechnology, for example. Governments have a role to play in monitoring their actions and reassuring the public that food is safe. Without regulation, some fear that these companies could hold us all to ransom by controlling food supplies from the seed through to the market.

Personal choices

As food consumers we can influence future food supplies in a number of ways. Some suggestions are listed on the next page, but by now you probably have your own ideas.

Urban agriculture is increasing as a means to grow more food. This small plot is in suburban Narita, Japan.

VIEWPOINTS

'Many hunger experts believe that ultimately the best way to reduce hunger is through education. Educated people are best able to break out of the cycle of poverty that causes hunger.'
United Nations Children's Fund

'They are sent to school without supper the night before and they may also miss breakfast. Standards decline if you are teaching a hungry child; a hungry child cannot learn.'
Emmanuel, head of primary school, Uganda

- Only buy what you will eat to cut down on food wastage.
- Buy locally to support farmers and reduce the distance food travels (food miles). Better still, try growing your own food if you can.
- Think about buying organic produce to improve the environment.
- Buy Fair Trade (or TransFair USA) products for which farmers have been paid a proper price.
- Join a group involved in the campaign to eliminate world hunger (see page 62).
- Tell others what you now know about food supply so that they can make choices too.

These grazing lands in Australia have became useless following a long period of drought. Climate experts predict that global warming could lead to similar problems around the world.

A changing climate

One issue that may affect future food supplies is our changing climate. Pollution from human sources has altered the composition of gases in the atmosphere and begun a process of global warming. Scientists warn that this may cause more extreme weather events, such as floods and droughts, and could alter growing seasons in many countries. The exact effect on food supplies is not yet known. Globally the effect may be minimal, but some of those areas that already suffer from local food shortages, such as large parts of sub-Saharan Africa, could find that their situation deteriorates further because their environments are particularly sensitive to climate changes.

Organic produce, on sale here in London, is becoming more popular but yields are lower, so what will it do for food supplies?

A hunger-free world

At the World Food Summit in Rome in 1996 governments agreed to try to halve world hunger by 2015. At the beginning of 2001 too little was being done to be sure of meeting this target on time. And this is only a minimal target. Many insist that we should look beyond this to make sure that people are self-reliant in food supplies and receive a balanced diet. With so much to be done, the early part of this century is unlikely to see an end to hunger. But by the time your children reach your age now, let us hope we will have succeeded in meeting everyone's right to have enough to eat.

GLOSSARY

agroecology agricultural practices that mimic natural ecosystems to encourage greater productivity.

biotechnology manipulating natural species for human gain. Includes cross-breeding of plants and animals (hybridization) and, more recently, modifying genes using genetic engineering.

Blue Revolution a term used to describe the expansion and development of fisheries (especially fish farming) as a source of food supplies.

bunds small ridges created to help conserve water and/or prevent soil erosion. They are often used across sloping land where erosion and run-off are greatest.

carrying capacity the total population that an ecosystem can support without being damaged.

cash crops crops that are grown to sell for money. They include crops such as coffee, sugar cane, and fruits such as apples and oranges.

contour ploughing a method of ploughing horizontally along the contours of the land instead of vertically up and down slopes. It has been proven to reduce soil erosion and help retain water.

deforestation the removal of trees, shrubs and forest vegetation. This can be natural (due to forest fires, typhoons, etc) or a result of human action, for example logging, ranching, construction, land clearance.

desertification a condition whereby soils lose their fertility. This can be due to topsoil loss because of erosion or the removal of vegetation, or as a result of intensive agriculture practices that fail to give soils time to recover between growth cycles.

developed countries generally wealthier countries of the world, including those of Europe and North America, Japan and Australia and New Zealand. People living there usually benefit from good health and education and are well fed.

developing countries generally poorer countries of the world, sometimes called the Third World and including most of Africa, Asia, Latin America and Oceania. People living there often suffer poor health and education and work in agriculture and lower-technology industries.

drought a long period of below-average rainfall that can lead to crop failures and water shortages.

ecosystem the contents of an environment, including all the plants and animals that live there. This could be a garden pond, a forest or the whole of planet earth.

eutrophication a process whereby water becomes enriched with nutrients which encourage rapid algae and plant growth. It can result in mats of plant growth blocking out the sunlight and starving the water of oxygen, leading to the death of aquatic animals.

Fair Trade products for which producers are paid a fair (and often guaranteed) price for their produce. Coffee, tea, bananas and chocolate are among the Fair Trade products available in many supermarkets. The equivalent non-profit monitoring organization in the USA is TransFair USA.

farmer-saved seed seed that is saved at harvest time for replanting in the following growing season (rather than buying new seed every season).

food deficit a shortage of foodstuffs in relation to the recommended food needed.

food security the ability to provide or obtain sufficient food to meet recommended amounts.

food surplus a surplus of foodstuffs in relation to the recommended food needed.

genetic engineering the manipulation of the genes that make up all living things. Used in biotechnology and to produce GM crops and foodstuffs.

global warming the gradual warming of the earth's atmosphere as a result of carbon dioxide emissions and other greenhouse gases trapping heat.

GM foods foodstuffs that have had their genes changed (genetically modified – GM) in order to improve their productivity.

Green Revolution the introduction of High Yield Varieties (HYVs) of wheat, rice and other cereal crops that began in the 1960s.

hydrological a term meaning 'relating to water'. Normally used in relation to the 'hydrological cycle' – the circulation of water as a result of weather patterns (rain, evaporation, etc.) and geographical processes (infiltration, etc.).

HYV crops High Yield Variety (HYV) crops are specially bred in laboratory conditions to produce higher yields than existing varieties.

Industrial Revolution the period in the late eighteenth century and early nineteenth century (150-250 years ago) in Europe when new machinery and the use of fossil fuels to generate energy led to the start of modern industry and dramatic changes in the way people lived.

intercropping growing several crops together in such a way that each benefits the other (as plants do in natural ecosystems).

irrigation a system of watering crops to make up for low or unpredictable rainfall.

malnutrition deficiency in the nutrients that are essential for the development of the body and for its maintenance in adulthood.

mono-cropping a system of farming in which a single crop is grown on its own. This is the basis of modern intensive commercial agriculture.

nutrient deficiency a shortage of a particular nutrient such as a mineral (e.g. iodine) or a vitamin (e.g. vitamin A or C) that can result in specific health problems.

obesity the condition of being clinically overweight.

organic farming farming or raising livestock without using artificial chemicals. Yields are often lower, but organic produce is said to be safer for human consumption and less damaging to the environment.

resources the materials and energy used in making products or providing services. Resources can be thought of as ingredients.

rotational cropping a farming system in which fields are planted with different crops in alternate seasons in order to avoid the declining soil fertility associated with continual farming with the same crop.

salinization a process in which mineral salts become highly concentrated in water or soils, affecting plant growth and in extreme cases causing land to be abandoned.

self-reliance the ability of an individual, family or country to provide for itself, either directly (through production) or indirectly (through purchasing).

subsistence farming farming that provides food mainly for the household, although surplus food may be sold.

terminator technology a technique that makes seeds infertile so that they cannot be replanted.

transition countries the countries of Eastern Europe and the former Soviet Union that are making the transition from planned to free-market economies like those of the USA and Western Europe.

vitamin supplements pills or capsules taken in addition to the normal diet to ensure that the body receives the correct amount of essential vitamins.

BOOKS TO READ

Earth Watch: Feeding The World
Brenda Walpole and Sally Morgan
(Franklin Watts, 2000)

Sustainable Future: World Food
Sally Morgan and Pauline Lalor
(Franklin Watts, 1997)

Food Matters
Gillian Powell
(Evans Brothers, 1998)

The World Reacts: Famine
Paul Bennett
(Belitha Press, 1998)

USEFUL ADDRESSES

http://www.enviroliteracy.org
A website searchable by topic, including food as a key category. Provides its own information files, with hotlinks to further sources.

http://www.fairtrade.org.uk
Information and contacts relating to Fair Trade foods and other goods. Education resource for teachers and parents wanting to learn more.

http://www.fao.org
The website of the Food and Agricultural Organization. Well organized for access to wide range of material, though not yet with a specific facility for younger users.

http://www.wfp.org
The homepage of the World Food Programme. Visit the newsroom for up-to-date information about hunger and food aid. You can also apply for a free 'hunger map' for your school.

http://www.thehungersite.com
A site that donates food to the world's hungry every time it is visited – visit each day and help fight hunger.

http://www.soilassociation.org
An organization campaigning for organic food and farming. Information and further contacts for anything relating to organics.

http://www.wwflearning.co.uk
World Wide Fund for Nature's learning site, with topical stories relating to global food supplies. User-friendly and informative.

Sustain: The alliance for better food and farming
94 White Lion Street
London N1 9PF, UK
Tel: 020 7837 1228

The Fairtrade Foundation
Suite 204
16 Baldwins Gardens
London EC1N 7RJ, UK
Tel: 020 7405 5942

WWF-United Kingdom
Panda House
Weyside Park
Godalming
Surrey GU7 1XR
UK
Tel: 01483 426 444

TransFair USA
52 Ninth Street
Oakland, CA 94607
USA
Tel: 510 663 5260

WWF-United States
1250 24th Street, N.W.
Washington DC 20037-1175
USA
Tel: 202 293 4800

INDEX

Numbers in **bold** refer to illustrations.